# Time Management

Verified Strategies For Efficient Time Management, Establishing A Routine, And Adopting Intelligent Work Habits: Comprehensive Handbook For Optimal

Time Management

**Stewart Benson**

# TABLE OF CONTENT

The Enhancement Of Time Management Through The Cultivation Of Positive Habits ....... 1

Supplements And Medication ............................... 23

Effective Strategies For Enhancing Time Management Proficiency ......................................... 54

The Relationship Between Time Management Skills And Achievement ............................................ 77

Simplify By Planning In Advance ....................... 142

Why You Put Off Things ......................................... 150

# The Enhancement Of Time Management Through The Cultivation Of Positive Habits

Mastering the art of managing one's time is undoubtedly an arduous endeavor. Distinguishing between matters of immediate importance and those crucial to one's overall well-being can prove to be a perplexing and intricate task. The capacity to discern between these entities proves advantageous in the context of matters pertaining to health. The complexity lies in the fact that, typically, the fundamental component of one's well-being often lacks a sense of immediacy in the context of health concerns.

For instance, though the necessity of attending the gym may not appear pressing to you presently, it unquestionably holds significant importance for your overall well-being in the long run. An additional illustration would involve the fact that experiencing stress in the present may not have a detrimental effect on your overall physical well-being. However, failure to address the root causes of this stress can potentially lead to a detrimental descent towards adverse circumstances. Ultimately, the consumption of processed food, fast food, or ready-to-eat meals will not significantly impact your emotional well-being, but it will significantly heighten the likelihood of developing physical ailments. Within this particular framework, it is of utmost importance to diligently allocate and oversee your time in order to ensure the maintenance of a nourishing diet and proper self-care as you embark upon the path to achievement.

## Focusing on Physical Health

This particular category presents a unique duality, representing both an area of relative simplicity and one of considerable complexity to effectively concentrate on. It is straightforward in the sense that it solely requires engaging in regular physical activity and maintaining a balanced diet. It poses a challenge as there exists a scarcity of individuals who actively develop and adhere to a comprehensive strategy to address their physical welfare. This is primarily attributable to our perceived inability to allocate sufficient time to maintain a proper diet and engage in physical activity.

When considering your exercise regimen, begin by dedicating yourself to engaging in 20 minutes of physical activity each day. This can encompass a range of activities, including engaging in morning yoga sessions or embarking on a brief 20-minute stroll following dinner. The crucial aspect is to derive enjoyment and gradually integrate physical activity into your daily regimen. Ensure that you discover an activity that not only brings you pleasure, but also possesses the capacity for daily engagement. Direct your attention towards an endeavor that lends itself to a seamless commencement while maintaining a stringent adherence to a procedure of high standards.

As one becomes accustomed to allocating dedicated time for physical exercise, it becomes possible to gradually enhance both the duration and the level of intensity of the exercise. Engaging in regular physical activity is an excellent means to minimize stress, enhance mental clarity, and maintain overall well-being, thereby preventing burnout.

Maintaining a nutritious diet is essential in order to effectively manage stress and prevent exhaustion. Consuming a nutritious diet comprising of fresh produce such as fruits and vegetables, proteins, and wholesome fats contributes to an enhanced well-being compared to solely relying on processed or fast food for sustenance.

In terms of maintaining a nutritious diet, engaging in proactive meal planning and carefully documenting your grocery list can contribute to ensuring personal responsibility. As you strategize your weekly meal preparations, it is crucial to incorporate ample quantities of fruits and vegetables, proteins, while controlling the intake of carbohydrates. Engaging in advance meal planning can help you economize time and prevent succumbing to the allure of ordering fast food during your evening commute.

Focusing on Mental Health with Meditation

Meditation offers a multitude of evidenced advantages, with its most renowned and extensively recorded implication being the augmentation of tranquility. This heightened state of tranquility can profoundly enhance your overall well-being and bolster your resilience in dealing with stressful situations. When individuals acquire improved stress management skills, they can effectively contribute to the moderation of their heart rate, reduction in blood pressure, and diminished cortisol levels in the body.

Engaging in morning meditation fosters mental and physical concentration, promoting a state of relaxation prior to commencing daily activities. If one is confronted with stress arising from projects, clients, deadlines, or other facets of their business, engaging in meditation can effectively redirect their focus away from these concerns prior to commencing their day.

Engaging in consistent meditation can also facilitate the attainment of a more optimal life equilibrium and act as a safeguard against exhaustion. Numerous individuals, including those involved in entrepreneurial endeavors, hold the belief that one must dedicate sixteen hours a day to diligently toil in order to lay the foundation of their business and achieve prosperity. Although the attainment of a prosperous business necessitates substantial effort and unwavering commitment, sustained prosperity mandates the harmonization of professional endeavors with a holistic approach towards one's personal life.

An increased propensity for burnout is likely to correspond with a diminished likelihood of achieving success. Nevertheless, maintaining equilibrium in various aspects of your life can foster triumph, not only in your professional endeavors, but also across different dimensions of your existence. The more proficient you become in time management, the greater amount of time you will possess for attending to your mental and physical well-being, consequently mitigating the risk of experiencing burnout.

What To Delegate

Do not assign tasks that you are incapable of handling.

Avoid assigning tasks that can be eliminated altogether. If engaging in a particular activity is deemed inappropriate, it would be advisable to refrain from assigning the same activity to others. Eliminate it.

Assign mundane tasks to others, even if it may not be your preference, as an example:

Fact-finding assignments

Production of preliminary drafts of reports.

Analysis of the issue and recommended courses of action

Acquisition of data for the purpose of generating reports

Photocopying, printing, collating

Data entry

Outsource tasks that fall outside of your fundamental area of expertise. For small enterprises, these encompass a range of services such as accounting, website design, deliveries, hardware maintenance, software assistance, graphic design, travel coordination, patenting, legal matters, and even human resources functions like payroll management.

There are certain tasks that cannot be assigned to others: conducting performance evaluations, enforcing discipline, terminating employment.

Develop a strategy for assigning tasks to others. Exercise discretion when assigning tasks.

Allocate a brief period of time to training in order to achieve a substantial long-term enhancement in productivity.

Others may possess the capacity to achieve superior results compared to your own abilities or discover novel approaches to accomplish a particular task.

Delegate, don't abdicate. Another individual can perform the assignment, however, you continue to hold accountability for its completion and for overseeing the delegation procedure.

Things to keep in mind...while delegating

Ensure that the criteria and the desired results are clearly defined. What tasks are required, by when must they be completed, and to what extent of quality or level of detail?

Assign the goal, not the method. Please articulate the intended outcomes rather than the specific approach.

Kindly request individuals to submit progress reports. Establish provisional deadlines to assess the progress.

Allocate the task to the appropriate individual. Do not always allocate tasks to individuals solely based on their strength, experience, or availability.

Facilitate the distribution of delegation tasks and provide individuals with novel experiences as a component of their training.

Acquire feedback from employees to ascertain that they perceive themselves to be treated fittingly. A straightforward inquiry such as "What is the current progress of the new project?" may suffice.

Ensure proper delegation of authority along with corresponding responsibilities. Please refrain from requiring individuals to return to you excessively for minor authorizations.

Place trust in individuals to perform satisfactorily without incessant surveillance or frequent follow-ups, unless they specifically seek guidance or feedback.

Anticipate the need to sacrifice instantaneous setbacks in favor of enduring achievements in the long run.

Once you have concluded imparting the necessary directions, it is advisable to inquire, "Is there anything further that you require to commence?" They shall duly provide the information.

Provide commendation and constructive feedback upon the completion of the project, along with additional tasks or responsibilities.

# Delegation as a Process...Procedure entailed in Delegation

Prior to commencing, let us comprehend the different obstacles in the process of delegation.

The primary impediment to delegation lies in surmounting the entrepreneur's affliction, wherein they persist in assuming complete responsibility for all tasks. That is a critical mistake that hinders the growth of start-ups, preventing them from becoming viable enterprises.

Here is a method to determine if you are progressively placing yourself at a disadvantage. When an acquaintance inquires, "What was the extent of your productivity at the workplace today?" would you respond by discussing your workload? Alternatively, do you prioritize the tasks that you have guided others to accomplish?

If you analyze the extent to which your employees are assuming additional responsibilities and alleviating my workload, that is an encouraging indication. It demonstrates that you are effectively entrusting tasks in a purposeful manner. However, when contemplating the multitude of urgent tasks that demanded your attention and the various crises you successfully resolved, it becomes evident that employing a more effective delegation strategy could be advantageous for you.

I advise caution when employing the subsequent justifications in order to evade the act of delegation:

1. The explanation is overly time-consuming. "It is a time-consuming task to provide an adequate explanation."

2. None of my staff members possess the necessary skills to accomplish this task."

3. In order to ensure the task is executed correctly, one must undertake it themselves."

4. My workforce is already operating at maximum capacity. I am unable to burden them any further.

Which of the aforementioned statements have you utilized to justify your failure to delegate?

Despite the aforementioned justifications, it is apparent that your true motives for declining to delegate may be as follows:

1. I am at ease with carrying out tasks independently. If I were to relinquish that pursuit, I would consequently find myself managing my company in a

manner that does not align with my personal comfort."

2. As the owner of the company, it is ultimately my responsibility to oversee all operations."

3. What if the other individual makes an error? As a fledgling organization, it is imperative for us to avoid any errors due to our limited financial resources.

Can you contemplate any additional rationales as to why you do not allocate tasks as extensively as necessary?

Why you Should Delegate?

You liberate yourself to manage your business and comprehend the broader perspective.

1. You enhance the abilities of your employees, thereby increasing their value.

2. You foster a culture of accountability to promote the development of a more robust and resilient team.

3. When your business is supported by agile employees whom you can trust, you have the ability to promptly adapt to changes and respond effectively.

"Delegation encompasses three components:

1. Responsibility

2. Authority

3. Accountability

When engaging in delegation, you allocate responsibility and authority to others while upholding their accountability for their performance. Nonetheless, the ultimate responsibility rests in your hands.

## Supplements And Medication

Pharmaceuticals and dietary supplements may not be suitable for all individuals, especially those who are currently undergoing a prescribed medication regimen. In such cases, it is imperative to seek prior medical consultation before introducing any new pharmaceuticals or supplements into one's diet. However, when feasible, the utilization of pharmaceuticals and supplements can contribute to cognitive acuity, enhanced mental acuity, heightened memory function, and overall physical well-being. These factors collectively play a pivotal role in maximizing productivity in professional settings.

Piracetam

Piracetam is widely regarded as a highly recommended supplement for enhancing productivity in professional settings. In contrast to prescribed medications, Piracetam is classified as an over-the-counter drug and has been employed for enhancing cognitive abilities since 1978. Piracetam belongs to a group of supplements commonly referred to as racetams. Racetams exert their effects by activating the acetylcholine receptors in the brain. Piracetam effectively enhances concentration, facilitates memory retrieval, augments response times, and heightens responsiveness to stimuli by stimulating heightened acetylcholine activity in the brain. Furthermore, Piracetam, a racetam compound, possesses the added advantage of alleviating anxiety, thereby enhancing the productivity of individuals who may otherwise experience hinderance due to anxious emotions.

Dopamine Supplementation

Prescription drugs that enhance productivity through the modulation of the neurotransmitter Dopamine necessitate constant supervision from a healthcare practitioner. Having made that observation, it can be noted that for individuals experiencing dopamine impairment, such medications can offer transient enhancements in productivity through heightened concentration and energy levels. The activation of dopamine receptors in the brain proves to be an ideal solution for certain individuals experiencing difficulties in achieving productivity. However, it is imperative to bear in mind that such pharmacological interventions entail accompanying adverse reactions. If you believe that a prescription dopamine supplement such as Ritalin or Adderall might be necessary, it is important to engage in a thorough consultation with your physician regarding the advantages and disadvantages associated with their usage. It is imperative to engage in conversations regarding the utilization of these categories of medications with employers on certain occasions. This is due to the fact that while they may enhance performance, they can also elicit adverse outcomes that can pose challenges in professions such as that of a 787 pilot.

Circumin

Circumin constitutes a naturally occurring element present within the spice known as Turmeric. Circumin possesses a multitude of noteworthy attributes, including antioxidant, anti-inflammatory, antibacterial, anti-viral, anti-cancer, and antifungal properties. Additionally, it has been observed to elevate serotonin and dopamine levels, facilitate the degradation of cerebral plaques linked to certain neurodegenerative conditions, and augment cerebral blood circulation. Each of these actions and attributes play a part in enhancing brain health, consequently leading to heightened levels of productivity.

## DHA

DHA, known as docosahexaenoic acid, holds significant importance as a dietary supplement for the human brain, to such an extent that it is frequently incorporated into infant formula. DHA, an omega-3 fatty acid, is a fundamental component involved in the construction of the cerebral cortex, which is accountable for various cognitive functions such as attention, creativity, language, neural signaling, motor skills, and memory.

## Citocoline

Citocoline is a chemical that is present within the human brain. It assumes diverse functions such as mitigating inflammation, curtailing free radical-induced harm, bolstering cerebral energy, promoting neural plasticity, enhancing concentration, sharpening attention, fostering laser-like focus, and elevating endogenous levels of dopamine and acetylcholine in the brain. It is noteworthy that citocoline has long been employed as an adjunctive therapy by European physicians in the management of neurological disorders.

## Acetyl-l-Carnitine

Acetyl-L-Carnitine, also referred to as ALC, exhibits antioxidant properties that safeguard the brain from free radical-induced harm. Acetyl-L-Carnitine (ALC) exerts its effects on the brain by enhancing brain cell sensitivity to insulin, thereby facilitating the efficient utilization of glucose for optimal brain cell functioning. In addition to functioning as a natural anti-depressant, ALC effectively enhances mood, promotes mental clarity, and improves memory. Enhances concentration abilities and augments cognitive processing velocity. The aforementioned traits, coupled with ALC's rapid efficacy, render it an ideal choice for enhancing productivity.

## Ginkgo Biloba

For an extended period of time, Ginkgo biloba has been employed in the realm of traditional medicine for its potential to enhance blood circulation, as well as to provide protection to the brain from oxidative stress caused by free radicals. Over the course of numerous years, ginkgo has been purported to possess the capacity to enhance memory. Nonetheless, recent investigations have unveiled that this assertion may lack veracity. Regardless of the veracity of this statement, it is undeniable that the cardiovascular and antioxidative attributes of ginkgo remain advantageous, thus rendering it a commendable supplement for enhancing overall efficacy.

Vitamins

In an ideal scenario, it would be preferable if everyone consumed a meticulously diverse diet that negated the need for a multi-vitamin supplement. However, it must be acknowledged that our current reality falls short of this ideal. In actuality, our dietary intake primarily consists of grains, sugars, and proteins, whereas fruits and vegetables comprise a minimal portion. Despite occasionally consuming fruits and vegetables, there is a consistent lack of diversity in our choices and they are typically prepared in a manner that diminishes their nutritional content. Therefore, it is imperative that we integrate a vitamin of superior quality into our daily dietary intake.

You might be curious as to the connection between the consumption of a daily vitamin and your capacity for being productive. The solution lies within a well-balanced diet, along with the incorporation of vitamin D and vitamin B. For our bodies to operate at their best capacity, they necessitate specific vitamins and minerals that provide nourishment to cells, tissues, and organs. In the absence of sufficient quantities of these vitamins and minerals, we start to exhibit symptoms of insufficiency. The manifestation of symptoms pertaining to vitamin deficiencies varies depending on the specific vitamin in question. However, there are certain deficiencies that have a tangible influence on cognitive function, subsequently impacting productivity.

- The B complex vitamins play a pivotal role in averting cognitive decline, safeguarding against memory impairment, fostering cognitive acuity, and facilitating the synthesis of neurotransmitters.

- Vitamin C, commonly known as the "cognitive-enhancing nutrient," has been scientifically linked to the improvement of memory, enhancement of IQ levels, mitigation of age-related cognitive decline, and inhibition of cortisol synthesis, a stress-related hormone.

- Vitamin D plays a crucial role in mitigating the cognitive decline linked to the aging process, enhancing problem-solving aptitude, and bolstering memory function.

- Vitamin E is reputed for its part in supporting cardiovascular well-being, yet it is additionally frequently employed to uphold cognitive wellness. Vitamin E exhibits significant efficacy in mitigating age-related cognitive decline.

- Vitamin K plays a pivotal role in preserving cognitive acuity and enhancing memory, notably in regards to verbal retention.

Employ this instructional manual to overcome the habit of delaying tasks

Upon uncovering the various underlying causes of procrastination, one may experience a sense of disappointment or become intrigued to delve further into the subject. If you choose the latter option, it offers the most advantageous position to be in, as this book will provide guidance on overcoming it. The aforementioned were merely a handful of strategies for effectively addressing each instance of procrastination. Subsequently, subsequent chapters will delve more profoundly into strategies for conquering procrastination. Prior to proceeding, it is imperative that we acknowledge a fundamental truth: we all exhibit tendencies of procrastination. It is inherently ingrained in our genetic makeup. It would be advantageous for us to promptly acknowledge and embrace this reality. We can progress beyond this situation and initiate the search for effective remedies. We are interconnected in this venture, and this book will assist you in embarking on a trajectory that enables the attainment of your utmost significant objectives. Given that we have come to acknowledge our collective tendency toward procrastination, let us now proceed to embark upon our path and delve into strategies for effectively managing our precious time.

A Call to Overcome Procrastination: Embracing the Cold Shower Approach

I would suggest attempting this exercise on your next morning shower. Procrastination arises from our reluctance to venture beyond our comfort zone and expend the necessary effort. We are disinclined to tolerate challenges and instead favor simplifying tasks. This phenomenon can be rationalized by the presence of two distinct shower knobs in your bathroom, specifically designed to regulate the temperature of the water—namely, one for hot water and the other for cold water. Hot water represents a space of utmost comfort and contentment where you often find yourself spending a significant portion of your time. Activating the hot water supply proves more convenient for you, as it imparts a pleasant sensation while standing beneath a soothing stream of warm water. Might I suggest attempting to manipulate the cold water faucet instead? You may experience a momentary pause, arising from an inherent apprehension of the inevitable - the contact of ice-cold particles against your skin, potentially leading to freezing sensations.

Your task entails abstaining from warm showers for a minimum duration of one week. I am simply instructing you to engage in the activity for a duration of 7 days. The initial attempt may prove challenging; you might spend up to thirty minutes merely attempting to manipulate that lever. Nevertheless, persist and overcome the inclination to delay. The objective of this activity is to develop a proficiency in embracing and adapting to feelings of discomfort. By actively engaging in self-imposed challenges and pushing beyond the boundaries of your comfort zone, you reduce the propensity for procrastination and cultivate a mindset that prioritizes prompt and diligent task execution.

This activity proved to be effective for me. I used to hate cold showers but when I challenged myself and tried cold showers for a week. To be candid, the initial two days were exceedingly unpleasant. It was an uncomfortable experience being subjected to a frigid shower. Subsequently, over the course of a few days, it began to gradually lead to a greater sense of comfort, thereby alleviating any initial discomfort. I have successfully acclimated to the discomfort, and as a result, cold showers invigorate me, fostering a more proactive approach to my mornings compared to the past. I am confident that you will experience a similar outcome. Please attempt this task.

Common Justification

A pivotal discovery regarding procrastination is that individuals who engage in this behavior tend to rationalize their actions, or rather, their lack thereof. The individual coping strategies for dealing with procrastination often lean towards avoidance or emotion-focused approaches rather than problem-solving or task-oriented approaches. The purpose of emotional coping is to effectively alleviate the stress associated with procrastination. This form of rationale affords an individual with gratification and affords them the opportunity to divert focus from the repercussions.

The subsequent are frequently employed methods that individuals employ to justify the postponement of their assigned tasks.

Valorization, or the promotion of enhanced achievements: An individual highlights their present accomplishments instead of dedicating their efforts towards a task of potentially greater significance.

Evading: An individual steers clear of the circumstances or vicinity where the task is being carried out. This does not constitute a verbal rationale, but rather a physical one. They take active measures to physically ensure their absence, which allows them to assert that they were unable to attend to the task. They may opt to refrain from attending meetings or elect to indulge in television rather than tidying their bedroom.

Laziness: This does not mean the person is lazy, because they are not. The individual who engages in procrastination is justifying their behavior by attributing it to a lack of motivation.

Diversion: They engage in alternative activities or behaviors as a means of avoiding cognizance of the task at hand.

Denial: They feign that they are not engaging in procrastination as they believe the task they are currently occupied with is of greater importance than the one they are deliberately avoiding.

Minimization: They attempt to persuade themselves that the task at hand holds little significance.

Rephrasing: They feign disregard for initiating a project promptly and neglect their tasks until the eleventh hour, under the misconception that it will yield exceptional results.

Comparisons: They draw parallels between their current circumstances and a more adverse situation.

External Attribution: They attribute the cause of their procrastination to external factors that are outside their sphere of influence.

In a light-hearted manner, individuals employ humor as a defense mechanism to evade expending the necessary effort in order to complete the task at hand, joking about their apparent lack of accomplishments and tendency to postpone their obligations.

Procrastination and Neuropsychology

In recent years, research into procrastination has advanced beyond the realms of personality, cognition, and emotion, encompassing the field of neuropsychology. It is widely acknowledged that a multitude of frontal brain systems are engaged in various cognitive functions pertaining to self-regulation, encompassing self-control, problem-solving, and planning. All of these fall under the category of executive functioning. Curiously, however, there had been no prior endeavor to examine a correlation between these cerebral regions and the phenomenon of procrastination.

According to Laura Rabin, an expert from Brooklyn College, it is quite remarkable that past studies have not thoroughly investigated the correlation between executive functioning components and academic procrastination, considering the crucial role of executive functioning in the inception and accomplishment of intricate behaviors.

In order to address this issue, Rabin and her colleagues assembled a group of 212 participants and conducted a comprehensive examination of their propensity for procrastination. Afterwards, they conducted an evaluation encompassing the nine distinct dimensions of executive functioning, namely: overall tidiness, cognitive retention, emotional regulation, attentive awareness, behavioral initiation, cognitive flexibility, strategic organization, self-assessment, and impulsive tendencies. The researchers engaged in this study anticipated discovering a correlation between specific subscales and the tendency to procrastinate. The procrastinators, as it transpired, demonstrated a noteworthy correlation with each of them.

Rabin provided an elucidation on the constraints of the study. Initially, it should be noted that their findings were merely correlative in nature, thus giving rise to uncertainty regarding whether the executive functioning elements can be conclusively identified as the root cause of the procrastination phenomenon. Additionally, the researchers incorporated numerous self-reports in their evaluations. It is possible that functional imaging may be necessary at a certain stage to augment or validate the observed delay within the brain's central region in real-time. This finding could potentially indicate that procrastination might be a manifestation of subtle impairment in executive functioning among individuals without any neurological disorders.

## Effects

It is of considerable importance to thoroughly examine the repercussions of procrastination. The repercussions individuals face as a result of squandering their time and failing to meet deadlines have a detrimental impact on both their personal and professional realms. The act of delaying tasks is prone to engender heightened levels of stress, diminished personal efficacy, a pervasive sense of urgency and remorse, and the potential for social and professional disapprobation stemming from the failure to fulfill one's obligations. The confluence of these emotions facilitates the exacerbation of procrastination.

Certain individuals may be driven to action by the stress and anxiety elicited by procrastination. Nevertheless, individuals typically proceed by endeavoring to provide rationale for their inclination to postpone their actions, thereby fortifying this conduct. The act of procrastination is often seen in individuals to a minor extent, but to fully eradicate this behavior, one must surpass the tendency to downplay or rationalize their actions as tolerable.

Among certain psychological communities, it is postulated that chronic procrastination may be indicative of an underlying psychological condition. Many individuals perceive procrastination as a valuable means of discerning one's true priorities, as it is uncommon to delay tasks that evoke genuine passion or interest.

Nevertheless, it is crucial for individuals who tend to procrastinate to acquire the skill of enhancing the significance of their inclinations, even if they do not derive satisfaction from them, enabling these inclinations to retain their worth across all facets of their lives. The widely held perspective on procrastination posits that task avoidance stems from a lack of drive, self-discipline, and accountability. Although individuals who study procrastination are aware that this assumption is incorrect, it remains the prevailing perception among the general public.

Interventions

As our comprehension of procrastination expands, researchers envision a heightened impact resulting from an intervention. Through the examination of executive functioning, various potential solutions for undesired delays might arise. Individuals who tend to postpone their tasks could enhance their ability to handle them efficiently by fragmenting their substantial assignments into more manageable components. Therapeutic intervention may assist individuals in recognizing instances where their pursuit of immediate gratification hinders the attainment of their long-term objectives. According to the research conducted by Klaus Wertenbroch and Dan Ariely on the phenomenon of "precommitment," devising an individualized timeframe proves to be highly effective. In an article published in Psychological Science in 2002, the scholars documented that individuals prone to procrastination successfully employed self-imposed deadlines, ultimately facilitating task completion. These categories of deadlines may not exert as significant an impact as externally imposed ones, nonetheless, they do provide assistance.

Addressing the affective aspects of procrastination presents a greater difficulty in terms of resolution. Strategies to overcome temptations involve eliminating sources of distraction; however, the challenge lies in the exertion of self-regulation, a quality often lacking in individuals with a tendency to procrastinate. Sirois contends that identifying a beneficial or positive aspect of the task is among the most effective approaches to alleviate the inclination to seek instant mood enhancement.

Ferrari desires a shift towards incentivizing punctuality rather than imposing penalties on tardiness. Amidst the various proposals he put forth, he communicated the notion that there ought to exist an incentive for filing taxes in advance, wherein individuals who file prior to March 15 would receive a tax reduction. Furthermore, he posits that it is imperative to cease facilitating the habit of procrastination in the context of interpersonal connections. While employing a firm approach in interpersonal relationships may prove beneficial, self-forgiveness serves as a paramount remedy for the well-being of an individual.

Ultimately, the act of procrastination is minimally associated with indolence, but predominantly linked to the predominant influences of evading tedious tasks and impulsive behavior. The majority of individuals possess the ability to discern procrastination as they engage in it. Individuals have the capacity to engage in introspection regarding their intended or necessary actions, subsequently providing rationale for their lack of progress towards these objectives. Procrastination tends to occur most frequently when we neglect to exercise control over impulsive behaviors and lack the necessary discipline to regain focus.

Fundamentally, procrastination occurs when we allow immediate emotional gratification to sway our motivations, rather than prioritizing the unpleasant emotional consequences associated with the tasks at hand. It is essential to comprehend diverse strategies for modifying our emotional intensity towards specific objectives in order to surmount procrastination and enhance productivity.

## Effective Strategies For Enhancing Time Management Proficiency

1. Strategizing and Allocating Resources 2. Organizing and Ranking 3. Establishing a Framework for Action

The process of strategizing holds utmost significance in effective time management. The act of meticulously strategizing one's tasks and objectives holds significant importance as it provides a well-defined understanding of the anticipated outcomes and the timeline for their accomplishment. Develop a strategic objective and divide it into more manageable daily undertakings.

## 2. Applications designed to enhance productivity

There exist a multitude of tools that facilitate the completion of tasks with increased efficiency and expediency. As an illustration, an interior designer is able to save time by utilizing software that streamlines the process of developing and designing floor plans. A business proprietor or a manager can enhance their work efficiency through the delegation of projects and effective utilization of specialized tools, thus allowing them to oversee the entire team more effectively.

## 3. Automation

Engage in the utilization and manipulation of information technology systems, machinery, and automated entities. It can be demonstrated that implementation of automation technology yields a substantial enhancement in productivity rates on both national and organizational scales. This concept can furthermore be extended to the realm of home automation. As an illustration, contemporary appliances such as a washing machine are often overlooked, as they effectively relieve us from engaging in laborious chores.

4. Methods for enhancing efficiency

The selection of a strategy that leads to increased efficacy, productivity, and prosperity while minimizing time consumption. For instance, an entrepreneur who possesses an imperfect strategy can swiftly waste several years.

## 5. Waste

Minimize unproductive time by effectively eliminating superfluous activities. This could necessitate modifications to one's lifestyle. Minimizing diversions may appear straightforward, however, it stands as a highly effective and efficient approach to acquiring additional time to dedicate towards your ventures or loved ones.

Time-consuming pursuits encompass any activities that are unrelated to one's objective.

5. "Establish explicit goals:

In the absence of well-defined objectives, it is imperative to allocate time towards comprehending one's true desires. Create a catalog comprising the various elements that bring you contentment, followed by a strategic plan encompassing the diverse endeavors needed to achieve the ultimate objective.

6. Execute Singular Tasks Sequentially

Rather than contemplating your next move, maintain your concentration on your current task. If you divert your attention towards multitasking or lack focus, you will become the primary impediment to your own progress.

7. Relax

It is important to acquire the knowledge of effectively managing one's work and leisure time in order to recuperate both mentally and physically following a prolonged work session. Taking regular breaks and ensuring adequate rest are crucial for increasing productivity in subsequent work sessions. It is important to bear in mind that a successful day is initiated by the preparations made the previous night.

Chapter 3:

What strategies can be employed to conquer the habit of procrastination?

By adhering to all the recommendations I have provided thus far, you are making commendable progress towards surmounting procrastination. Nevertheless, there are additional steps you can take to further assist you in achieving your goals.

11. Eliminate all sources of diversion. The presence of distractions may vary depending on the specific task and location in which it is being conducted. Allow us to deliberate on the tasks that I was required to undertake. I previously mentioned that I work remotely, however, what I failed to disclose is that I am the parent of three children and the

owner of two canines. My children receive their education through home-based instruction, ensuring their continual presence alongside me. Naturally, our canines also remain in constant proximity. My approach to addressing this matter involved the conversion of an available room into my designated workspace. During the periods when the children are engaged in their chores or assignments, I can dedicate my entire focus to my work undisturbed, unless an instance arises where a dog enters my workspace seeking to be let outside. This period holds great significance for me, and it took me some time to acquire the skills needed to optimize it properly.

I was utilizing this period of the day as a personal respite, engaging in computer gaming, film viewing, and overall relaxation. Subsequently, once my children had completed their tasks and obligations, I would encounter a sense of urgency to fulfill my own responsibilities. However, the predicament arose that I now had to contend with famished and unoccupied children who required both amusement and attention. What was the primary source of my diversion? FACEBOOK.

Please refrain from passing judgement, as it is a common challenge faced by many individuals who work remotely. You might observe that our professional engagements predominantly take place in virtual environments, as opposed to direct dealings with fellow adults.

12. Please remove and prevent access to all Facebook games. Remove any software on your computer that is causing distractions. This activity is preselected as your default option. When experiencing boredom or uncertainty regarding your next course of action, it is common for individuals to revert to their default activity. If Facebook is proving to be a distracting influence on your work, it may be advisable to completely remove it from your digital landscape. If it is necessary for your professional responsibilities, retain possession of it, but restrict the duration of its utilization. Additionally, you have the option to acquire extensions for Google Chrome which enable you to restrict access to particular websites throughout your designated work hours. I have

determined that this was highly advantageous.

13. Please ensure to review your email in the morning and evening. While checking your email can serve as a default task, it is important to assess the necessary frequency for doing so. Is it truly necessary for you to allocate five minutes of every hour to perusing emails and subsequently an additional five minutes for checking your Facebook account? It will require an additional duration of 10 minutes for you to transition back into work mode; consequently, you are effectively achieving only 40 minutes of actual work within each hour dedicated to work. Avoid or minimize the use of email and Facebook during working hours, whenever feasible.

14. The manner in which you commence your day will determine the course it takes. If you initiate your morning with a tranquil and unhurried pace, engage in a few recreational activities, peruse your electronic correspondence, and allocate some moments to unwinding. This will establish the rhythm for your day. Please reserve such activities for the evening when you have leisure time available.

15. Prioritize the most challenging tasks. Yep, that's right. A common challenge faced by many of us is the tendency to prioritize easier tasks at the start of the day, leaving the more challenging ones for later. The proper course of action is to prioritize the most challenging tasks and complete them first. When we postpone the most challenging tasks, we often discover rationales to avoid

tackling them and postpone them to a subsequent day. Similar to prioritizing activities that bring us pleasure and postponing those that seem mundane, this tendency hinders our ability to fulfill our obligations and subsequently heightens our levels of stress.

16. Determining your peak energy levels and maximizing productivity within that timeframe is paramount. The majority of individuals demonstrate enhanced productivity during the morning hours compared to the post-lunch period. Consequently, it is advisable to allocate approximately 80 percent of your workload to the former timeframe.

An additional aspect to consider is the potential benefit of investing in a laptop, particularly if you are engaged in remote work. This would afford you the flexibility to relocate from your office and make use of various spaces within your home, or alternatively, venture outdoors, thereby facilitating greater productivity in your work. I have observed that while I am capable of accomplishing a substantial amount of tasks throughout the day, I experience discomfort with the notion of idleness. Thus, I ensure that I have my laptop with me during the evening hours. This allows me to efficiently accomplish a few tasks while the family is engaged in watching television, enabling me to make progress in advance for the upcoming day. Naturally, the outcome will be contingent upon the nature of the task at hand and the level of attentiveness it necessitates. From my perspective, I am confident in my ability to undertake assignments that are not excessively intricate in nature. For instance, I am capable of transcribing handwritten documents for a client in a casual setting such as a living room.

17. And thus, I arrive at this suggestion. Make the most of all of the time you have. While I may hold the opinion that multitasking is not an effective method for increasing productivity, I do comprehend the circumstances under which one might feel inclined to refrain from leisure activities like watching television in the evening, as they may be driven by a desire to complete pending tasks. Therefore, ensure that you are fully capitalizing on every available hour within a given day.

Consider this. To what extent will you expend valuable time by idling in front of the television or engaging in other purposeless undertakings that hold no potential for personal or interpersonal betterment? Would you be able to eliminate these activities from your life and engage in pursuits that will potentially bring about personal growth and benefit?

18. Numerous individuals engage in procrastination due to a dearth of motivation to accomplish the tasked obligations. In this particular scenario, it is imperative to ascertain the benefits that you stand to acquire by successfully fulfilling the task at hand. Recall the instance when I mentioned that individuals tend to engage in activities solely when they anticipate receiving

some form of compensation. It is imperative to ascertain the compensatory benefits that shall be accorded upon task completion. In my experience, I recognized the necessity of engaging in daily work, regardless of circumstances, and it gradually became mundane to me. I recollect reclining in my bed one evening, contemplating the immense contentment I experienced during the initial phase of transitioning to a work-from-home setup. I pondered upon the item or items that I had misplaced. I had misplaced the prize. I had momentarily neglected the experience of seldom glimpsing my offspring due to their consistent presence in educational institutions or under the care of child minders. I had momentarily lost sight of the experience of relinquishing a significant portion of my hard-earned income to compensate a babysitter for tending to my children during their slumber. Upon adopting this perspective, a shift in circumstances became apparent.

Subsequently, I was obliged to proceed with dismantling it into individual tasks. I was compelled to devise a strategy to consistently empower myself and accomplish every task. I discovered that motivation when I fell behind in my financial obligations. I realized that unless I promptly devised a solution, I would be compelled to revert to employment beyond the confines of my residence. I had intended on delegating the task of managing my schedule and determining my daily earnings to someone else. I would have been obliged to allocate fifty percent of my income towards remunerating a childminder, consequently rendering it infeasible to continue educating my children within the confines of our residence. Motivation found.

It is imperative to allocate a period of reflection wherein you can discern the underlying causes of your lack of motivation and ascertain the factors that will serve as catalysts for inspiring you. If it becomes necessary for you to commend yourself, it is permissible. Grant yourself modest rewards and observe the significant impact it can bring forth.

19. Take some time off. Yes that's right. An overarching cause of procrastination is excessive workload. When one habitually engages in a continuous cycle

of working seven days a week out of a perceived obligation, it is not uncommon for tasks requiring completion to be increasingly postponed. I would like to emphasize that my intention extends beyond discussing solely professional responsibilities, but also encompasses the idea of undertaking domestic tasks within one's personal residence. We all require periods of respite, and I recommend that you designate one day per week as non-working. Utilize your time engaging in leisure activities, finding enjoyment, and cherishing the company of your loved ones. This provides you with a goal to strive for on a weekly basis, while also affording you the opportunity to alleviate mental clutter. Over time, you might discover that you will be exerting more effort throughout the weekdays in order to secure the opportunity to enjoy a single day of rest or even to indulge in a two-day respite over the weekend.

Once again, I encountered difficulties with this matter. Please have faith in my words as I express that I faced immense challenges with procrastination; rather, it would be more apt to convey that I endured significant hardships due to it. It constituted a consistent struggle. I dedicated around 12 to 14 hours per day to tending to my children and managing household affairs. I was effectively accomplishing only six hours of work per day. The reason behind it was my fatigue. I would often postpone tasks due to fatigue. Due to fatigue, I would occasionally neglect the completion of tasks. I experienced a sense of disorientation, however, upon reducing my working hours and days, I achieved a surprising increase in productivity and even managed to indulge in occasional days of leisure.

20. This leads me to the final recommendation of this chapter, which is to ensure that you are obtaining an adequate amount of sleep. Engaging in procrastination leads to increased levels of stress in one's life. When one experiences stress in their life, it is common to face difficulties in achieving restorative sleep. When faced with difficulties in attaining sufficient sleep, one tends to engage in procrastination. It is a terrible cycle that you have to get out of and it starts with getting enough rest. Having adequate rest enhances one's energy levels, ultimately fostering increased motivation and enabling the

completion of tasks more efficiently. You are more inclined to avoid procrastination as you will be aware of the constraint, which prohibits working on the project during late evening hours.

## The Relationship Between Time Management Skills And Achievement

As we embark upon this chapter, allow me to provide a word of caution. Undoubtedly, we have all been familiarized with the various adages concerning the importance of empathetically envisioning ourselves in the positions of others. This is an occasion in which such action should be refrained. Do not aspire to emulate an individual solely based on their perceived success. You are not aware of the extent of sacrifices that individual made in order to attain such remarkable success. That individual might observe and express a longing for a family. So, are we clear? Exclusively focus on self-reflection and deliberate on your personal aspirations and desires in accordance with your priorities.

What is success anyway? The characterization of success is contingent upon the individual being queried. My conception of success primarily revolves around the aspects of family and overall existence. The notion of success held by some individuals revolves solely around their professional pursuits. Thus, let us examine the precise definition and analyze its contents. The accurate interpretation can be stated as follows: "The genuine meaning can be summarized as the favorable or prosperous culmination of efforts or undertakings, the achievement of one's objectives; the acquisition of wealth, status, accolades, or similar accomplishments." Given this particular definition, individuals who perceive success as being connected to familial and personal aspects, much like myself, and those who perceive it as being linked to one's professional endeavours, are both validated in their perspectives.

It is contingent upon your priorities and values.

Now, for the purposes of discussion, let us presume that your success lies in the realm of your professional pursuits. You display a keen focus on professional commitments and possess a strong aspiration to maximize your achievements in your chosen profession. You seek to ascertain the most effective application of time management techniques in achieving this objective. Very well, let us now proceed to examine several approaches to accomplishing this task. Please be advised that the scope of our discussion is solely limited to time management specifically pertaining to tasks and activities carried out by individuals.

Initially, allow me to express this. It is essential to bear in mind that success lies in working intelligently, rather than exerting excessive physical effort. Putting in greater effort in no manner implies an increase in productivity. You may exert tremendous effort but achieve no tangible outcomes. This occurrence is a regular and frequent phenomenon. Individuals who fall within this classification are at high risk of becoming ensnared in a perpetual cycle of unproductive labor. Therefore, it is imperative to adopt efficient working methods, which encompass making judicious decisions regarding time management. Furthermore, it is imperative to consider the following: time is a universal factor that remains constant for all individuals, and regardless of one's financial status, the acquisition of additional time is an unattainable feat. The length remains consistent for each individual, and the commencement and conclusion are identical for all. Individuals who achieve success invariably retain these two fundamental principles in their consciousness. They exhibit efficient work practices while being conscious of the irretrievability of time.

Dale Beaumont, the esteemed founder of Business Blueprint, presents a collection of enlightening seminars on the subject of time management that can be accessed conveniently through online platforms. Within one of his recorded sessions, he deliberates upon the crucial matter of efficient time utilization, and subsequently illustrates his point by offering a practical scenario. Upon listening to his speech, it evoked in me recollections of my own practice of multitasking during toothbrushing, though he appeared to be connected to the realm of business. He suggested utilizing the travel time in the car as an opportunity for contemplation and strategizing. He further alluded to Parkinson's law, which posits that the amount of work undertaken tends to expand in correspondence to the amount of time allotted for its completion. In the event that there are individuals who require additional elucidation on this matter, the notion being conveyed is that the duration of your work tasks will be commensurate with the extent to which you permit them to endure. This phenomenon exhibits both advantageous and disadvantageous aspects, contingent upon the manner in which it is employed.

The initial recommendation pertaining to the utilization of time management in fostering a thriving professional trajectory is to consistently engage in daily planning, ensuring the commencement of each day is contingent upon the completion of said planning. Ideally, it would be advisable to make the arrangements either during the preceding day or evening, conceivably during quality time spent with the spouse, albeit discreetly. Pre-arrange your daily schedule. Make arrangements for your week ahead. Pre-arrange your annual schedule. Increased levels of strategic planning result in higher quality outcomes. Now, let us consider the scenario where your day has been meticulously scheduled. It is now the appropriate time to commence our work. Let us proceed to explore strategies and initiatives that can effectively enhance our achievements.

Ideally, your career selection was primarily influenced by your skills and capabilities. Typically, individuals do not tend to opt for a profession that stretches their capabilities to the maximum, and even if they do, it is often short-lived. Consequently, you possess a level of self-awareness regarding your strengths and areas for improvement.

This does not solely pertain to the initial stages of your career but must be taken into consideration throughout all of your decisions that hold significance. Once again, presented is another exemplification of astute work practices. What course of action would be advisable in this situation? It's simple. When circumstances allow, it is advisable to assign tasks that are challenging or time-consuming for you to individuals who possess the capacity to complete them more efficiently and effortlessly. Within this context, it is necessary to evaluate the cost-benefit ratio. Make sure that the extra costs are warranted and prove to be more beneficial to the overall picture or task.

Another recommendation for achieving success in terms of working intelligently is to consider employing a proficient specialist with expertise in specific domains who can provide occasional assistance or impart knowledge on enhancing skills in those particular areas. If investing in the services of an instructor yields enhanced long-term efficiency, then justifying the additional expenditure becomes highly probable, simultaneously aiding in the optimization of time management. You allocate a reduced amount of time to one task, thus enabling the reallocation of that time to another. An illustration of the concept I am discussing pertains to an accountant engaging the services of a tax preparer during the duration of February until April, in order to handle uncomplicated tax returns for certain clients. This arrangement enables the accountant to allocate sufficient time towards resolving the more complex cases. This not only conserves the accountant's time, but also leads to monetary savings, as tax preparers can be remunerated at lower rates compared to accountants. Consequently, the overhead expenses per billable hour are minimized. Enhanced productivity is achieved with a simultaneous reduction in costs. This is a mutually beneficial situation for any enterprise that I am acquainted with.

Allocation of tasks, the act of assigning responsibilities and duties to an individual, coupled with both permanent and temporary outsourcing, plays a pivotal role in the prosperity and advancement of any enterprise. This extends beyond mere time management; it embodies fundamental principles. If the matter is not dictated by common sense, it undoubtedly ought to be. If one were to examine the schedule of numerous accomplished chief executive officers, it is highly likely that the sheer plethora of distinct responsibilities undertaken by them would be astonishing. Individuals who achieve success demonstrate their proficiency in effectively and judiciously assigning tasks to others, thereby maximizing the potential benefits derived from such delegation.

An additional recommendation for achieving success is to effectively utilize imposed time constraints, commonly referred to as forced deadlines. Allow me to mention that this is an aspect in which it is simple to make errors. We will get to that later, but I'm talking about one of the ugliest curse words known in business: procrastination. One should exercise caution and possess a sound understanding of business principles in order to avoid the temptation of procrastination. One effective approach to address procrastination is through the utilization of deadlines, as they effectively sustain a sense of urgency within one's cognitive processes. It enables us to consider points of culmination where our position at the forefront of the competition is crucial, with these points not solely limited to the ultimate conclusion of the endeavor or the conclusion of the day, but rather dispersed at various junctures.

Deadlines facilitate the encouragement of increased efficiency in one's actions and perspectives. You will experience a reduction in wasted time, enhanced progress and efficacy, and a bolstering of self-assurance. Furthermore, one could strive to elevate their performance by engaging in more challenging tasks. What distinguishes a forced deadline from a conventional deadline? I have no idea. That can be found in an alternative literary source. Naturally, it was merely intended as jest to ensure your continued focus. In all honesty, it can be likened to the distinction between a large apple and an exceedingly substantial apple. By imposing a predetermined cut-off point, the conclusion or time limit is established with the intention of expediting or enhancing the efficiency of the given task. You are planning to alter the present course of the task in order to enhance its efficiency or quality.

Okay. We have thoroughly examined strategies such as optimizing unproductive intervals, engaging in outsourcing, delegating responsibilities, subcontracting, providing training, implementing deadlines, and embracing other valuable insights for effective time management. Now, let us proceed to evaluate additional notions and recommendations provided by individuals with firsthand experience and a demonstrated track record of success. I would like to reiterate the crucial significance of identifying your objectives and bearing in mind that time is an invaluable and irretrievable resource, as it pertains to effective time management. It possesses single-use functionality, necessitating your informed judgment regarding its optimal utilization within that timeframe. In this aspect of life, it is imperative to prioritize your own desires and make choices based on personal preferences, rather than catering to the expectations or demands of others. Upon reaching the culmination of your existence, it is you who will be filled with remorse should you choose not to undertake this endeavor.

In the present juncture of this chapter, I shall proceed to elucidate an additional personal encounter that will serve as an exemplification of effective allocation of time. Previously, I discussed the emphasis I place on prioritizing my family above my professional endeavors, and how this value influenced my decision to resign from a position as general manager at a retail and rent-to-own establishment. I would like to present an additional illustration from my professional background within the aforementioned organization and role, wherein I acquired several valuable insights during my tenure. Astute and efficient entrepreneurs understand the significance of workforce management, and thus engage individuals who possess the competence and willingness to fulfill all assigned responsibilities, including those that may extend beyond the customary duties and prescribed delineations of their respective roles. In the event that you receive instructions from the management, it is imperative that you comply with them or contemplate seeking alternative employment. Management must be informed that once assigned tasks or additional responsibilities, you will diligently carry out the assigned duties and ensure their successful execution, with accuracy, productivity, and thoroughness. They desire for you to accomplish this autonomously, without constant guidance or supervision. If your reliability and dependability are lacking in the eyes of management, it is likely that your tenure with that organization will be limited.

The establishment where I was engaged as a franchisee. Nevertheless, the corporation possessed a distinct and meticulous staffing framework with a criterion established according to the volume of patrons specific to each store. As the store attracted an increasing number of customers, it necessitated a corresponding increase in staffing. As the general manager, I possessed the authority to both recruit and dismiss employees at my discretion. Therefore, in the event that I discerned that an employee failed to meet the required criteria, it was incumbent upon me to address the matter. I would accept full responsibility for an employee who adversely impacted the business, as it was within my capability to rectify the situation. The aforementioned issue entailed a laborious procedure in terms of recruiting and instructing individuals, which frequently led to a perception that it was more expedient to overlook inadequate levels of competence and productivity in employees.

At present, my employer encompassed a multitude of distinct establishments. My franchise comprised approximately 40 distinct retail establishments. I am solely accountable for any incidents or occurrences within my establishment. I received compensation whenever the store achieved exemplary performance. In the event of any issues arising within my store or a decline in business, it became my responsibility to be held accountable for such matters. Indeed, that was the determining factor regarding the duration of my tenure. A regular evaluation of all stores across various regions was conducted on a weekly basis. If your establishment maintained its position at the pinnacle of the rankings, you could be confident that your employment would be secure in the foreseeable future. My store retained its position at the pinnacle, and I harbored the intention of preserving its esteemed status. While my utmost commitment has always been to my family, I exerted my utmost effort in order to excel in my professional responsibilities. This culmination occurred several months into my tenure at that organization.

I held the belief that the recruitment of new personnel entailed greater difficulties, compared to simply turning a blind eye to the shortcomings exhibited by certain employees. I was cognizant of my accountability and the obligation to address any outcomes, positive or negative, pertaining to my establishment. Furthermore, it should be noted that my earnings were intricately linked to the financial prosperity of the establishment. Therefore, I was compelled to ensure utmost efficiency and profitability for my establishment, as ultimately, the financial outcome was the primary focus of my management. I opted to retain all the remaining particulars within the confines of the residence. This encompassed the allocation of personnel and the individual efficiency of each employee.

I employed an individual who displayed considerable intellect, yet unfortunately chose to direct their cognitive abilities in manners that were suboptimal. Initially, he was aware that regardless of whether he exerted significant efforts or merely fulfilled the minimum requirements to retain his employment, his compensation would remain constant. He was aware that my usual practice did not involve the termination of employees, owing to the challenges associated with recruiting and training replacements. Finally, he was aware of my lack of availability to monitor and ensure his diligent engagement in tasks. As a consequence of these circumstances, he exhibited a limited level of productivity, to the point of being almost negligible, without any exaggeration. He proved to be an exceptionally unsatisfactory employee, but I committed a grave mistake by severely compromising my time management skills. I undertook the responsibility of performing his duties in addition to my own. This grave error proved to be a regrettable misjudgment, resulting in my prompt entrapment within the relentless pattern of arduous labor that yielded meager output. In due course, he was discharged from his position and a replacement was subsequently appointed in his stead. Significant improvements ensued thereafter, and I made a solemn commitment to ensure that such circumstances would never transpire in the future. The concept I am endeavoring to highlight is the importance of not procrastinating or opting out of undertaking tasks solely due to their level of difficulty. If optimizing business operational efficiency is a priority, then it is advisable to proceed accordingly. The majority of managerial decisions, including this one, encompass the aspect of time management to some extent.

There are various aspects of time management that can be explored and numerous examples that can be employed for discussion. Nevertheless, I wish to avoid indulging in excessive discourse that could potentially be unproductive and time-consuming for both of us. This chapter focuses on implementing effective time management strategies to enhance business performance and productivity. I believe that we have sufficiently covered this. Allow me to provide a summary of our previous discussion.

Initially, it is crucial to bear in mind the elements that you perceive as your foremost concerns. Align your time management with your beliefs and priorities. Upon completion, you may proceed to the subsequent stage. Commence preplanning your day and refrain from initiating your day until the completion of said preplanning. Examine the periods of time during which you are not engaged in productive activities, and evaluate how you can incorporate additional tasks, such as the act of planning, to effectively optimize that time. When strategizing work responsibilities, opt for delegation or outsourcing as deemed most advantageous. Additionally, you have the option to engage in outsourcing in instances where it will enhance productivity and optimize time utilization. Apply prudent judgment in staff selection and refrain from procrastinating on tasks, even if they appear challenging or time-intensive. It is preferable to complete the task promptly and without delay. Set goals and prioritize. Enabling oneself to acquire knowledge from individuals who demonstrate expertise or greater intelligence in specific domains. Engage in diligent re-reading of both this chapter and the entire book until you have assimilated a significant proportion of the material therein.

The last point that will be remarked upon in this chapter pertains to the shared connection between accomplished individuals and their respective personalities. Just like any other aspect of a prosperous business, it is imperative to incorporate a degree of assertiveness. Individuals who possess assertiveness are inclined to achieve higher levels of success in various domains, including the realm of business. They exhibit great conscientiousness and unwavering determination in upholding their beliefs. They frequently assert their refusal; their determination remains steadfast and unwavering in pursuit of their intended course. Individuals with a pronounced disposition towards assertiveness tend to be predisposed towards assuming leadership roles rather than adopting follower positions. The aforementioned statement holds equal validity when it comes to time management, just as it does with the other components of the business. In the process of strategic planning, it is crucial to establish unambiguous and succinct objectives while maintaining resolute determination to pursue them relentlessly, demonstrating unwavering commitment and putting forth dedicated efforts. These attributes are pivotal for achieving success and effective strategizing. The skill of being assertive can be acquired or developed. Therefore, if you currently lack assertiveness, focus on developing this quality. It will greatly enhance time management efficiency.

This may be surprising, however, despite the extensive discourse on achieving life balance, incorporating a slight deviation into your daily routine can lead to significant benefits. I am making a reference to the principle of time management, commonly referred to as the Pareto Principle, which involves the concept of controlling 80% of outcomes through 20% of efforts.

Imagine yourself in the position of a Chief Executive Officer leading an organization with a dedicated team of sales professionals. In the present context, characterized by parity, it is reasonable to anticipate that each individual contributes to sales in a manner commensurate with the overall distribution. Specifically, 20% of employees are expected to contribute to 20% of sales, while 50% contribute to 50% of sales, and 80% are responsible for 80% of sales.

Regardless, it is important to contemplate the potential scenario where, instead of a one-to-one correlation, you come to realize that 80% of your sales are actually generated by only 20% of your employees.

This concept pertains to the phenomenon known as the 80/20 control, where the majority of effects in a given situation are derived from a small fraction, specifically 20%, of the underlying causes. This phenomenon was initially discovered by Vilfredo Pareto, an Italian economist, who observed that a minority comprising 20% of the entire population in Italy possesses a significant majority - 80% - of the wealth and property.

Upon careful observation and analysis, he noticed that a mere 20% of the peapods in his garden produced a significant 80% of the total harvested peas.

The 80/20 concept is commonly referred to as "The Pareto Principle" or "The Law of the Vital Few" which pertains to a select few factors that contribute to the majority of the outcome.

Listed below are several recent instances where the 80/20 principle can be readily observed:

Population: The vast majority, specifically 80%, of the population residing in England (amounting to 25.8 million individuals out of 32.3 million) can be traced back to a mere 20% of its urban areas (specifically 53 out of a total of 263 cities).

Resource Utilization: The utilization of 70% of the global energy resources, 75% of its metallic resources, and 85% of its timber resources is attributed to 20% of the world's countries, despite these countries having a considerably smaller portion of the overall global population.

Natural Resources: A significant majority of Earth's mineral wealth is concentrated within a comparatively small portion, comprising less than 20%, of its surface.

An unequal wealth distribution is evident, as a mere 10% of adults lay claim to approximately 85% of the total global resources.

Usage: Within every sector, a small fraction of brands dominate global consumption, for instance, Coca Cola/Pepsi for carbonated beverages, MS Windows for operating systems, Samsung and iPhone for mobile devices. (I provide additional information in The Market Leader Effect.)

Daily Routine: When dining outside, you frequently indulge in meals at the same establishments (20% from all available options).

In the business realm, it is observed that a significant majority, specifically 80%, of offers typically emanate from a select minority, approximately 20%, of clients. These esteemed customers display steadfast loyalty to your services or products, demonstrating their admiration through regular purchases. Approximately 80% of complaints arise from a select 20% of customers.

Interpersonal Connections: The majority of the regard one receives from associations emanates from a select 20% of individuals in their social circle, namely their close friends, family, and partner.

Objective attainment: The majority (80%) of the desired outcomes in your objective will be derived from a select few (20%) of the activities you engage in. This implies that a small number of key tasks will contribute significantly to the overall success of your goal.

The principle of Pareto's Law suggests that the correlation between input and output is seldom, if ever, in equilibrium. When implemented in a professional context, it signifies that approximately 20 percent of one's efforts yield 80 percent of the outcomes.

Deciphering how to perceive and subsequently prioritize that 20 percent is crucial for optimizing your time effectively. "Allow me to present you with a couple of expedient suggestions for fostering the principle of 80/20 analysis:

Conduct an examination of the overall populace in your vicinity. Approximately 20% of your partners, staff, and patients are likely responsible for delivering 80% of the support and fulfillment you seek. They are the initial supporters of your venture. Ensure their well-being is prioritized. Similarly, it is possible that you can identify several individuals within your circle of acquaintances who would stand by your side unconditionally. Please endeavor to prioritize them and avoid postponing their completion.

Look at your work. Reflect upon the query, "In what manner would I genuinely intend to pursue my life and allocate my time?" What aspect of my job would be prudent for me to focus on, accounting for 20 percent of my responsibilities?

Principle #1: Acknowledging the Power of Simplicity

From the very outset, it is evident that not all things possess an equal standing. Despite one's actions, there consistently exist a handful of significant tasks that hold significance. It is imperative that you focus your attention on the vital few, specifically the 20% of tasks that hold significant value, rather than attempting to cover a broad range of responsibilities.

This concept is commonly referred to as 'Less is more,' whereby achieving greater outcomes can be attained by engaging in fewer actions or exerting less effort. This equates to effectiveness rather than efficiency, a topic that I elaborate on in my blog posts regarding time management.

Implementing the principle of "Less is more" entails posing the question to oneself:

What is the most effective method for eliminating the projects that do not generate significant admiration?

How can I channel my energy into exercises that bring about increased joy and fulfillment?

## Chapter 08 Utilize Technological Advancements

The advent of technology has brought about a profound transformation in the contemporary world. Particularly, the domains of business and entertainment. The proliferation of communication and data transmission technology has significantly enhanced the efficiency and precision of information dissemination.


In the contemporary landscape of commerce, there has been a profound shift from the practices and dynamics observed in the previous century. In order to communicate the message, individuals would traditionally engage in the act of writing correspondence and mailing it. Subsequently, computers and emails were introduced, resulting in a significant reduction in the duration of communication. In contemporary times, individuals are significantly constrained by time, to the extent that composing emails has become a daunting task. A vocal recording is transmitted promptly even while operating a vehicle.

In today's world, one needs to run just to stay where he or she is, meaning just to stay in line with others. In order to maintain a competitive edge, individuals must exert greater speed and agility. We simply cannot afford to fall behind. It is imperative that we adopt technology across a spectrum of tasks, as failure to do so may result in us being disadvantaged and falling behind.

Technology plays a pivotal role in effectively managing time, particularly in the domains of:

Automation

Data transfer

Communication

Text correction, Edition

Storage and retrieval

Without a doubt, technology has facilitated our ability to connect, accomplish tasks, enhance performance, and maximize the utilization of our resources in ways that were previously unimaginable. One prominent example of this is the usage of time management applications. Given the multitude of applications available, how can one discern which ones are suitable to utilize?

To effectively discern an application, it is advisable to evaluate one's existing struggles pertaining to the management of time. Are you prone to frequent distractions, often hindering the completion of tasks? Alternatively, you may conclude the day with minimal accomplishments, pondering the allocation of your time throughout.

"Below, we have compiled a list of several technological tools that can be incorporated into our daily routines:

Some Technological Tools

Utilization of desk time: Facilitating seamless project management

The DeskTime project time tracker facilitates the establishment of practical deadlines, enhances the organization of both personal and team workflows, and aids in the estimation of future project durations.

DeskTime's Project feature allows you to estimate the potential costs of a new project. Issue a project, assign it to your staff members, and acquire the projected expenses based on the employees' respective hourly rates.

Cease the manual composition of project reports. DeskTime generates comprehensive reports that contain all pertinent project data, including individual employee productivity metrics and total project time allocation.

A formal alternative could be "****************************************.

Zoho People: It helps evaluates performance, elevate productivity, and exchange feedback. The principal domains of application encompass:

Employee Database Management

Attendance Tracker

Performance Management

Employee On boarding

Timesheets

Learning Management

Shift Scheduling

Case management

*****

It is expected that Rize will

Rize not only monitors your time but also provides you with valuable insights to enhance your productivity, cultivate superior habits, and enhance your concentration. The noteworthy aspect is that there is no necessity for continuous data input as this task is automatically undertaken on your behalf.

One can observe the number of hours invested, the portion of time dedicated to focused work, the extent of time spent in context switching, and the identification of the most distracting websites, among an array of other functionalities. It has become increasingly convenient to monitor and effectively administer your use of time.

Available on Desktop

*****

Concept - Maintain an Efficient Handle on All Your Tasks

Obstacle: Engaging in unproductive activities with various productivity tools.

The concept revolves around an integrated platform that houses diverse productivity applications, facilitating the consolidation of your notes and work within a unified location. You can collaborate, share documents and notes, and create a central knowledge base for your team, supporting you in all your project management needs.

One can utilize Notion as a viable alternative for managing one's to-do lists, project management tasks, note-taking activities, spreadsheet operations, and more. It aids in the optimization of time and financial resources, while facilitating effective time management and organizational endeavors.

Skill 16 - Manage Disruptive Thoughts

Distractions can arise from various origins, encompassing even one's own cognitive processes. Indeed, it is quite plausible that this could be deemed as one of the most detrimental forms of distraction given that, unlike the presence of a bothersome colleague, extricating oneself from its influence is considerably more challenging.

In order to manage interfering thoughts, the initial step is to dismiss or set aside them. Suppose you are engrossed in a project when, unexpectedly, an ingenious concept for the novel you have been crafting alongside it comes to mind. Rather than indulging in the notion, document the concept on a piece of paper and subsequently dismiss it from your mind. In due course, you can resume your engagement with it.

If you find yourself grappling with emotionally intrusive thoughts, it would be beneficial to schedule dedicated time for self-care or seek professional guidance from a therapist to facilitate your healing process. Recognize the notion, subsequently disregard it by reminding yourself that the present moment is not conducive for such considerations. Inhale deeply, thereafter exhale to expel it from your organism.

## Skill 17 - Engage in weekly self-assessment

Engaging in periodic self-assessment holds significant value. Engaging in this practice will facilitate your ability to enhance, modify, and even reevaluate your objectives.

Allocate a specific duration of 30 minutes to one hour during the weekend to critically assess the effectiveness of the time management techniques employed throughout the week. Please record the successful and unsuccessful attempts, thereafter contemplate alternative approaches that may prove more effective than the previously attempted ones.

Another factor to consider is the frequency of distractions encountered and the corresponding strategies employed to manage them. In the event that you encounter relevant distractions that prove challenging to circumvent, you now have the chance to effectively deal with them.

It is advisable to diligently document your self-evaluations for the purpose of utilizing them as points of reference in the development of future time management strategies.

Chapter 6: Applications for Enhancing Efficiency

Welcome to the dawn of an era where your mobile device can serve as a powerful tool to enhance your productivity. You may find it remarkable to discover the wide range of applications available nowadays, designed specifically to assist individuals in enhancing their time management skills. Presented herein are a selection of applications that are available to you without any cost whatsoever:

Focus Booster

The Focus Booster incorporates the Pomodoro Technique as described in the preceding chapter. It functions as a timekeeping device with enhanced capabilities, enabling efficient time management in brief intervals while mitigating the possibility of distractions.

One noteworthy aspect of this application is its ability to record sessions and present them in a thorough spreadsheet format, facilitating the opportunity for time analysis. Additionally, you can acquire recommendations on how to optimize your time utilization.

Rescue Time

Regrettably, Rescue Time does not come without a cost. On the positive aspect - it is undeniably a commendable application with a plethora of noteworthy features. This application is ideally suited for individuals who primarily conduct their tasks using digital platforms or computers, including PC, Linux, Mac, or Android systems. Rescue Time fundamentally monitors your computer usage and presents a graphical representation illustrating the amount of time allocated to various websites.

This enables users to ascertain which websites are deemed as unproductive or time-consuming. Significantly, it offers a genuine depiction of how one truly allocates their time, allowing for improved time management.

Any.Do

The Any.Do application, which offers an all-encompassing range of features, is particularly suited for individuals who frequently engage in collaborative endeavors. The primary advantage of Any.Do lies in its capability to allow the sharing of the list among individuals collaborating on a common project.

In addition to that, Any.Do encompasses the fundamental functionalities one would expect from a typical time management application. This encompasses shopping lists, task lists, written records, prompts, and scheduled occasions. Additionally, it is possible to synchronize the application with alternative devices.

Toggl

Toggly functions primarily as a tool for tracking and recording time. To accomplish this, it is recommended to activate and deactivate the device as needed while assigning suitable labels to facilitate its future utilization or retrieval. You also have the option to arrange chronological markers and employ this functionality to monitor billable hours for individuals who are billed based on time. It is presently among the applications employed by individuals engaging in remote work. Timesheets can be dispatched, exported, generated as hard copies, and appraised.

Calendar planners for task management

Electronic calendars offer superior efficiency by enabling users to effortlessly generate task lists and receive timely reminders prior to important deadlines. This encompasses the full range of capabilities offered by the application, spanning from data synchronization to task prioritization, and even the integration of Google Maps into your tasks.

Remember the Milk

Remember the Milk is a convenient application that facilitates the organization and management of your time across multiple devices. This functionality is compatible with both computers and mobile phones, offering seamless integration with popular applications such as Twitter, Google Calendar, and Gmail. In addition, it is possible to categorize task lists based on their respective priorities or their relevance to different domains such as home, professional, or educational contexts.

Time Doctor

This application serves the collective effort by assisting with time tracking, offering timely reminders, furnishing comprehensive reporting capabilities, and seamlessly integrating with additional computer networks. It possesses the supplementary advantage of monitoring sessions by means of capturing screenshots, thereby enabling you to ascertain the actual productivity of your employees. Regrettably, the application does not come at no cost.

Google Calendar

An offering from Google that is without cost, this Calendar provides a comprehensive task list accompanied by estimated start and completion times. You have the flexibility to include or exclude tasks as the process unfolds. One has the ability to add new tasks, schedule appointments, and allocate specific time slots for desired activities. One of the notable aspects of Google Calendar is its extensive cross-platform compatibility, allowing users to seamlessly integrate it into their mobile devices, tablets, and personal computers. In the event that you should misplace your electronic device, you may obtain access to your account from Google, ensuring that nothing is truly irretrievable.

Todoist

The Todoist, a time management application suitable for both individual and collaborative tasks, offers the capability to organize assignments, establish due dates, and receive timely notifications for pending activities. It facilitates the monitoring of critical assignments and enables seamless teamwork and collaboration within your team. It is accessible in multiple languages and can be synchronized across all your devices.

Focus @ Will

This application harnesses the synergistic influence of music and neuroscience to enhance and optimize productivity. The application fundamentally offers an uninterrupted stream of music that has been scientifically demonstrated to support brain function. Evidently, it is intended for application in intellectual pursuits such as administrative tasks or academic writing endeavors. For more mundane tasks such as household cleaning, though, its effectiveness may be limited. It is not provided free of charge, therefore it is necessary for you to take this into consideration.

Atracker

This personal time monitoring tool enables individuals to gain insights into their daily activities through a comprehensive reporting system. Users have the ability to personalize the settings of the tracker, incorporate additional tasks, and assess the ones already completed.

Evernote

Evernote is widely recognized as one of the prominent time management applications available in the current market. It can be utilized for the purpose of orchestrating, harmonizing, modifying, and securely retaining your tasks, facilitating universal accessibility. It operates primarily as a digital memo that can be accessed from any device.

If a certain condition is met, then a specific action will be executed.

Another distinctive time management product, it utilizes a fundamental logical principle whereby the execution of one action serves as a catalyst for engaging in another. This is the identical underlying principle employed in the "Rhythm Routine" elucidated in a preceding section. The application, nonetheless, employs the term 'recipe' and provides a plethora of pre-established and modifiable recipes. As an illustration, provided that you are present in the workplace, it is expected that you will switch your mobile device to silent mode. Provided that it is Friday, you must ensure to deliver your laundry to the dry cleaners. Furthermore, it is equipped with a GPS and Maps integrated To Do List feature. Therefore, in the event that you proceed to a specific location and your checklist encompasses a task that necessitates completion there, it would duly notify you of said task.

Naturally, these mentioned applications represent only a limited selection of the Time Management Apps available for download on Google Play at present. While a select few do require payment, a majority of them are accessible at no cost, provided that you opt for a straightforward upgrade that necessitates payment. Please consider exploring any of these options to assist you in managing your daily responsibilities.

## Strategies for Mitigating Catastrophes

Take a look at the measures you can implement to proactively mitigate the occurrence of disasters.

### Do It Right

Develop strategies aimed at increasing employment

To optimize the use of time in your home business, devise strategies that facilitate efficient workflow within your workspace. Establish a systematic and organized approach that ensures a step-by-step process is implemented, enabling one to progress from an initial stage to subsequent stages and beyond. Avoid restarting the process whenever a task requires your contribution.

Develop plans to address recurring tasks.

This would encompass any physical or digital resources that you would employ to advance the progress of your enterprise. Ensure a perpetual availability of sufficient provisions that can be easily accessed at any given time.

Make use of a calendar, whether in digital or physical form, in order to maintain a record of your scheduled appointments. You are prepared to observe the comprehensive schedule encompassing attire selection and necessary tasks for the day. This could potentially aid you in effectively organizing your day to achieve optimal outcomes.

Maintain a perpetually tidy workspace, with documents systematically organized and readily accessible, while continuously ensuring that the essential tools and resources relevant to your business remain within convenient reach.

Plan enough rest periods.

Sleep experts advise that the conventional, physically fit adult should aim to obtain a minimum of eight hours of sleep per night. This enables individuals to operate effectively and achieve high levels of productivity. However, according to a survey conducted by the National Sleep Foundation's 2000 Sleep in America omnibus poll, the average duration of sleep for adults during the work week falls just below seven hours.

Within the context of your organization, it is imperative to allocate an adequate amount of time for rest in order to optimize productivity. The extent of variation in quantity differs among individuals, and it is important to allow your body to determine the optimal conditions under which it functions effectively.

Certain individuals necessitate a duration of 8 hours, while certain individuals may require a longer or shorter period. Your physique acknowledges the remedy.

Develop your communication skills

Effectively and convincingly articulating your understanding through both spoken and written means is of paramount importance for the success of your business. Devote yourself to continuously enhancing your speaking and writing abilities. By opting for this approach, you will be able to efficiently manage your time while significantly enhancing your professional trajectory.

Learn To Delegate

Efficient time management relies heavily on the art of delegation. The ability to effectively assign tasks enables you, as a digital entrepreneur, to have the freedom and versatility to work on multiple projects concurrently.

Understand the appropriate timing for cessation

To enhance efficiency, ensure that you systematically set a reasonable and attainable timeframe for any assigned tasks that you delegate. Ensure that the delegation is equitable and impartial, and that it is manageable and feasible for the individual to whom you have been assigned. It is imperative to consistently communicate precise expectations when delegating tasks to avoid any ambiguity and ensure successful attainment of the desired outcomes.

When assigning tasks, ensure utmost clarity regarding the objectives of the delegated work and the desired outcomes that are expected. Exercise caution when assigning tasks without providing guidelines, as it has the potential to result in chaos, disorder, and subpar workmanship. If you are lacking the necessary time to provide the individual with comprehensive and clearly defined instructions, you may consider delegating the task to a person who can handle it with minimal supervision. This approach could prevent excessive involvement in minute details, allowing you to focus on higher-value tasks and enhance your overall productivity.

Consistently provide individuals to whom you have delegated with the opportunity to exhibit creativity in their tasks. Simply pursue and anticipate high-quality results without prescribing a detailed methodology for project execution. This undermines the overarching objective of delegation and is bound to generate unwarranted strain as well.

Create a plan to provide regular updates to you, in order to request feedback regarding the individual's progress. This prevents constant disruptions from occurring throughout the day. Maintain a record of significant dates to ensure regular acquisition of feedback. Kindly ensure to maintain a record of all assigned tasks and consistently update the record with any received feedback.

## Simplify By Planning In Advance

How to optimize your time usage

Engaging in proactive thinking can serve as the most effective approach to enhancing time management and efficiency. If you are concurrently involved in multiple activities, it is prudent to contemplate the optimal approach to accomplishing them. This straightforward measure can result in a considerable time-saving over an extended period. You may believe that you have insufficient time for this particular stage, yet it is fundamentally the most crucial step. Engaging in impulsive actions without proper consideration is unlikely to yield favorable outcomes. Devote ample time to considering and devising a well-thought-out strategy. Allocating a mere 10 or 20 minutes of your time is preferable to squandering hours on a task that could have easily been completed within minutes, had you exercised foresight.

On certain occasions, one may inadvertently commit to certain tasks prior to comprehending their full extent. Take the time to not only think about what you are going to do but also if you should even do it at all. Does it provide any advantageous outcomes for you? Will it potentially facilitate matters for you in any manner? Engaging in foresight can aid in preventing the occurrence of decisions that may yield unfavorable outcomes.

Isn't it evident that individuals who achieve great success consistently demonstrate a propensity for being one stride ahead of their peers? Indeed, that is the case. They always think ahead. They possess the ability to envision various potential outcomes of the situation and have devised a strategic plan for each contingency. They possess the awareness that meticulous planning is imperative for virtually every endeavor they undertake. With only a small investment of time, you too can emulate the achievements of those individuals who have attained remarkable success. It is essential to proactively anticipate future circumstances. Conceive the anticipated outcome of the situation and devise a strategic plan accordingly. In addition to envisioning the desired outcome, it is imperative to strategize for potential undesired outcomes as well. It is not an expression of negativity; rather, it signifies a state of readiness.

Presented herewith is an illustrative instance of the proactive approach pertaining to task management, whereby one endeavors to acquire control over impending assignments prior to their execution.

One can illustrate this point by considering the following example:

Envision a scenario wherein you are confronted with three tasks that necessitate completion on the following day. The dog requires grooming, and it is necessary for you to retrieve your dry cleaning.

It is necessary for you to purchase groceries.

It is evident that bringing your dog along is not permissible in establishments such as grocery stores or dry cleaners.

Taking him to be groomed, waiting for him to finish, and then returning him home would be a time-consuming endeavor.

Upon bringing your dog to the groomer, you may subsequently attend to the remaining two tasks during the grooming process.

There remain two tasks that require your attention during the dog's grooming session.

The dog grooming establishment and the Dry Cleaners are situated in close proximity to one another, with only a street separating the two facilities. It would be reasonable to prioritize retrieving your dry cleaning initially.

Subsequently, you may proceed to the grocery store to acquire the items on your list.

Once you have completed your task, it will be appropriate to fetch your dog and proceed towards your residence.

Rather than squandering half of your day endeavoring to accomplish these three tasks, you now have a significant amount of additional time at your disposal. Engaging in proactive thinking and strategic planning can significantly optimize time efficiency. Three tasks that could have occupied a considerable amount of your time have been amalgamated. You currently have an increased amount of time available to dedicate to other tasks.

This approach is applicable across all domains of your life, facilitating enhanced efficiency and effectiveness in the management of time. This skill can be employed for domestic cleaning purposes or during travel engagements.

For example:

Consider embarking on an international excursion. There may be certain items that you require but are unavailable at that location. Alternatively, you may encounter difficulties in locating nearby establishments in close proximity to your lodging. By proactively considering the future and conducting preliminary investigations, all of those issues can be eradicated. Obtain a map in advance. Kindly proceed to the currency exchange counter at the airport to convert your money. All of these factors will contribute to time-saving and enhance the overall enjoyment of your journey.

Given that you have now discerned your time-consuming activities and are anticipating future outcomes, improvement is certain to follow.

## Why You Put Off Things

Upon completion of the initial chapter, you will be equipped with a comprehensive understanding of the concept of procrastination.

It is an action that individuals have undertaken at some point in their lives, regardless of whether they acknowledge it. Whilst you are currently engaged in perusing this literary work, it is likely that there exists an underlying matter lingering in your thoughts, which you are intentionally delaying.

In instances where our negative emotions (such as self-doubt, fatigue, etc.) outweigh the positive ones (such as excitement and enthusiasm) with regards to a task, it is at that point that we succumb to the habit of procrastination.

We commence the undertaking at hand solely in the eleventh hour. We feel stressed and anxious and irritated with ourselves for not starting earlier…yet, when given the opportunity again, we still do not get to work on time.

If this resonates with you, there is no reason to presume that you are an anomaly. There are, indeed, numerous individuals who share similar characteristics to yours. Procrastination is an inherent aspect of human behavior. Nevertheless, the prevalence of this phenomenon should not imply that it is a situation that warrants acceptance or contentment. It is imperative that you make a sincere effort to eradicate it completely from your existence.

Consequently, the pivotal matter at hand revolves around devising effective strategies to overcome procrastination.

There exist numerous potential resolutions.

There exist expedient measures that yield short-term results, yet they do not prove effective over prolonged durations. One of these approaches encompasses the tactic of compelling oneself to engage in a specific task by rendering non-compliance inconvenient. For instance, let us consider the scenario where you have been postponing the adoption of a healthier diet.

Therefore, you allocate a considerable amount of money towards nutritious food and fully stock your refrigerator. Currently, you would rather consume the plentiful supply of vegetables residing in the refrigerator drawers, instead of allowing them to spoil and acknowledging the unfortunate reality that your diligently earned money is being squandered.

Although this approach can yield results in the short term, it is not a sustainable solution for the future.

An additional frequently employed approach that individuals resort to is initiating the task promptly. Suppose you have been delaying the task of cooking dinner, all you need to do is motivate yourself to initiate the process. You extract the meat and vegetables from the freezer and place them meticulously on the countertop. That's it.

Now that you have initiated this initial action, the subsequent progression appears noticeably less challenging than it did previously.

This, once again, nevertheless, represents merely a temporary resolution. It fails to address the underlying complexities of procrastination, hence my presence here to provide you assistance in this regard.

## Understand the procrastination cycle

One may have observed that when engaging in procrastination, there is a distinct pattern, or cycle, that their thought process undergoes.

The phenomenon of procrastination can be likened to a sentient force, akin to a formidable entity (as previously elucidated), which operates autonomously without regard for its consequences on an individual's well-being.

The aforementioned cyclic phenomenon was expounded upon in a most articulate manner within the literary work entitled 'Procrastination: Why you engage in it, and the appropriate measures to ameliorate it' authored by Jane B. Burka and Lenora M. Yuen.

The process commences with your reception of a task that necessitates completion, alongside an assigned deadline for its execution. This task may be either self-assigned or delegated by another individual. In any case, it is imperative for you to undertake this task.

Upon receiving the assigned task or determining the necessity to carry it out, you promptly resolve within yourself that you shall refrain from engaging in procrastination this time. On this occasion, you will commence your task with utmost expediency and deliver exceptional results within an accelerated timeframe.

After the passage of five minutes, followed by five hours, and subsequently five days. You have yet to commence the task at hand. At this juncture, you might be contemplating, "Although there is ample time left, it would be prudent to commence my efforts promptly."

You swiftly conclude that today, indeed, is the day. Today, you will commence the task with great zeal.

The morning transpires, followed by the progression of the afternoon. Time flies, and soon enough, it is well past midnight.

At present, initiating the task would be deemed untimely, would it not? You come to the conclusion that prioritizing sufficient sleep is of greater importance. You will commence work on the assignment tomorrow morning. In order to alleviate the intensifying unease, you convince yourself that you will awaken at an exceptionally early hour of four in the morning, with the intention of commencing work on the matter.

However, once your eyes awaken, it is already midday.

The subsequent phase of the cycle entails self-questioning, and the initial fervor and zeal have waned into insignificance.

You sense a growing sense of apprehension taking hold of you, prompting introspective pondering on the potential consequences of perpetually failing to commence the assigned undertaking.

You invest, or perhaps I should state, squander, your time envisioning the alarming repercussions that would ensue in the event of your failure to accomplish the assigned task.

Innumerable insignificant musings commence to infiltrate your cognition, impeding your ability to initiate proceedings even at this moment. It is highly likely that your prevailing sentiment revolves around remorse. You regret your excessive procrastination. You desire that you had commenced two days prior, or at least one day earlier!

In order to alleviate the negative ruminations regarding the job you are disregarding, you commence showing an inclination towards alternative tasks that hold significantly lesser significance. For instance, one might opt to rearrange their wardrobe or tidy up their living space as a means of diverting their attention from the imminent deadline that approaches steadily.

Individuals engage in this behavior with the intention of experiencing a sense of productivity and achievement. They are, without a doubt, accomplishing a task; however, it is an unnecessary endeavor that fails to measure up to the significance of what they are failing to attend to.

Nevertheless, there are individuals who abstain from utilizing this approach. Certain individuals opt for what could be considered a suboptimal choice, engaging in activities that provide temporary entertainment and distraction, resulting in a squandering of time. This might entail activities such as attending social gatherings, indulging in extended film or television marathons, immersing oneself in a consecutive collection of novels, engaging in extensive conversations via text, and so forth.

Although it is indeed factual that engaging in these actions may provide a fleeting sense of relief, the subsequent emergence of an unpleasant sensation of guilt, akin to a sinking feeling in one's stomach, will undoubtedly manifest each time one recollects the imperative responsibilities left unaddressed. You may additionally encounter emotions of self-revulsion, which not only proves to be a negative encounter but also poses a psychological risk. Engaging in this experience frequently has the potential to undermine one's self-assurance and self-worth.

An additional consideration that may enter your mind at this juncture is the experience of shame and humiliation. You actively employ stringent measures in order to safeguard the fact that your delay in commencing the task remains concealed from all individuals within your acquaintance. This may entail feigning productivity in relation to the task at hand, such as the act of consistently opening the assigned textbook whenever your roommate enters the room, appearing fully engaged with its contents. Subsequently, once the room-mate vacates the room, you revert to squandering time.

You consistently devise the most extravagant justifications for individuals, engendering a profound sense of disconsolation due to the mendacity of your assertions. This is another factor that may potentially lead to a decline in self-confidence.

The subsequent phase of procrastination involves engaging in elaborate rationalizations, supported by meticulous calculations, in an attempt to persuade oneself that there remains a viable opportunity. If I commence working on the task precisely 1.22

minutes from now and abstain from sleep for the subsequent 48 hours, I will be able to complete it two minutes prior to the designated time for submission.

Despite your attempts to cultivate a positive and optimistic mindset, you are still unable to commence with your tasks.

In the subsequent phase, one significantly escalates the level of intensity experienced within the self-deprecatory apparatus. You exhaustively explored all available strategies, but regrettably failed to accomplish the necessary task. At present, the sole deduction that can be made is that the issue resides within oneself, implying a potential inferiority in comparison to others. This particular idea has the potential to lead to significant harm and can instill a profound sense of despondency.

Presently, there are two possible outcomes.

One could opt for the alternative approach of avoiding the task entirely, succumbing to feelings of overwhelming stress and guilt, deeming them insurmountable.

One might be inclined to believe that further efforts are futile, prompting the question of the purpose behind attempting to proceed. It would perhaps be more advisable to relinquish our efforts, wouldn't you agree? Wrong.

While it would have been more desirable to have abstained from procrastination from the outset, given that you have already reached this juncture, it is imperative that you persevere and exert maximum effort.

In this concluding phase, harness the accumulated pressure and channel it constructively. Utilize it to compel oneself to initiate the task, and subsequently persevere until its completion. You may realize that this isn't as bad as you had expected, and this thought can be used to push yourself to get started earlier next time.

After gaining a comprehension of the procrastination cycle, let us proceed to subsequent sections where we will delve further into comprehending and overcoming procrastination.

Regard procrastination as the malevolent force that I have consistently depicted it as in various instances throughout this book. An adversary that necessitates conquering.

In order to defeat a highly proficient adversary, it is imperative to have a thorough understanding of their capabilities and weaknesses. It is imperative to possess knowledge of their weaknesses and strengths in order to strategically determine the most effective approach for prevailing over them.

This book is facilitating the accomplishment of that objective.

7

Starting from Step One

Time represents the invaluable currency of your existence. You possess a singular coin, and exclusive authority rests with you to determine its utilization. Exercise caution, lest others assume responsibility for such actions on your behalf.

—Karl Saibagh

The largest expedition commences with a preliminary stride. This concise proverb possesses inherent significance. Initially, it is advisable to commence the process of careful contemplation. Subsequently, it may come to your attention that there are aspects that have previously eluded your consideration. Occasionally, our initial understanding of a task may not accurately reflect the actual requirements until we commence its execution.

Throughout the examinations, we are confident in our ability to succeed. The process of revising will greatly augment one's levels of confidence. During the process of revision, our focus should be directed towards the most important inquiries. Compile the pertinent and significant questions from the previous year's question papers.

Create a comprehensive master worksheet containing all requisite tasks. In addition, it is essential to create a daily worksheet encompassing a comprehensive list of tasks and activities to be accomplished on that particular day. Whenever you are in the process of preparing the sheet for the given day, kindly retrieve it from the principal document. Please remove from the master spreadsheet any tasks that have been finished.

The timing at which you experience a surge of energy is contingent upon your circadian rhythm. One must comprehend their circadian rhythm and subsequently devise a suitable schedule. Commence the process of reviewing material a month in advance of the examination. This methodology aims to bolster levels of self-assurance.

The question bank will consist of a multitude of questions pertaining to the syllabus. Through the diligent application of these practices, one can effectively encompass the entirety of the syllabus. Within the confines of the examination venue, students are allocated a period of three hours. In order to successfully finish the question paper within a duration of three hours, efficiency and promptness are paramount. In light of this, during the process of revision, it is crucial to possess a keen sense of timing.

Approach the examination as a comprehensive undertaking or treat it akin to a project. Establish an objective and diligently pursue it. In the absence of a designated objective, one may experience a sense of aimlessness and subsequently encounter fatigue. Consequently, you cease your efforts without attaining the intended outcome.

In order to achieve a satisfactory performance on the examinations, it is imperative to implement effective time management strategies. It is advisable to prioritize attempting the questions that pose less difficulty. Based on the queries presented, it is necessary for you to allocate and disclose the allotted time. Don't give more time to one question which appears to be known to you.

Relationships and Love

If the objective is to effectively balance relationships and academic pursuits, acquiring skills in time management proves indispensable. Create a timetable and subsequently organize all the tasks accordingly. Kindly communicate to your partner the importance of time and encourage their focus on academic pursuits. In order to effectively navigate and cultivate relationships and romantic connections, it is essential to prioritize and devote attention to one's own personal growth and well-being. During the period of examinations, it is imperative to prioritize one's academic pursuits over romantic relationships. Upon the conclusion of your examinations, you are permitted to engage in romantic activities.

Effective management of one's time is crucial in ensuring the completion of any given task. You are encouraged to prioritize your work and effectively address any urgent matters, ensuring minimal disruption to your work schedule and ultimately achieving success in both endeavors.

Weekly Review

Conducting a periodic assessment, while adapting to the circumstances, is also considered a strategic approach. On a weekly basis, or specifically on Sunday evenings, it is advisable to conduct a thorough examination and assessment of your notes, tasks, and schedule. During the preparation of the weekly schedules, it is important to give due consideration to the elapsed time and the duration of the available examination period.

It is advisable to cultivate the practice of commencing study sessions by focusing on the most challenging tasks or subjects. If you are operating at maximum efficiency, then you will experience a heightened sense of revitalization when engaging in those tasks.

While you still have pending academic tasks, it is advisable to refrain from indulging in tasks that can be deferred. This could potentially be regarded as one of the most arduous tests in the realm of time management. As individuals engaged in the process of learning, we are susceptible to becoming drawn to alternative pursuits, thereby compromising our diligent preparation for examinations or other tasks. When exam, work, etc. Alleviate stress by minimizing external distractions that impede focus, thereby increasing the potential for experiencing greater contentment. Think with self—respect. Instead of expressing a negative response, it is advisable to adopt the phrase 'at a later time'.

Consider that period during which you have the opportunity to acquire a significantly limited amount of knowledge. Similar to utilizing public transportation such as buses. Perhaps you are engaged in the study of music or acquiring knowledge of grammar particular to different languages. What would be the optimal occasion to listen aside from the moment of commuting home by bike after school?

It is possible that you are currently in queue for a particular purpose. This presents an ideal opportunity to review the material you have read or undertake a lesson review. The utmost priority lies in effectively utilizing the available time.

In the early hours of the morning, ascertain the tasks that need to be attended to. Prior to retiring for the night, engage in the practice of mentally organizing your tasks and obligations for the ensuing day.

Utilize a monthly chart as a means of premeditated planning for forthcoming events. Thoughtful organization and strategic scheduling of your time will be meticulously arranged to facilitate effortless recollection.

Some Best Practices

Prepare some daily schedules. Prepare them prior to retiring for the night or in the early hours of the morning upon awakening. Through this, you will become acquainted with the specific actions you will embark upon throughout the course of the day. Allocate a specific timeframe for each task.

Please establish a designated timeframe for all tasks. It is imperative to ensure that the first task is completed by 10 o'clock, the second task by 2 o'clock, and the third task by 5 o'clock. By utilizing this, your tasks can be completed punctually, eliminating the necessity of sharing time slots.

Use a calendar. The utilization of a calendar is paramount in effectively organizing and overseeing daily tasks and obligations.

Focus on deadlines. Please record a specific target date on your calendar by which you intend to finish your tasks. Please ensure that every task is accomplished within the designated timeframe.

The objective is predetermined with a flexible timeline, allowing for potential completion ahead of or beyond the set timeframe. However, if the deadline is approaching, it will be completed within the designated timeframe. When you have scheduled an appointment with someone, it entails the expectation of being present at the designated location prior to the agreed-upon time.

It is essential to consistently monitor the passage of time. Ensure that you have a watch in your possession. Frequently, we become so engrossed in our tasks that we inadvertently lose awareness of the passage of time. Therefore, efficient time managers must possess a timepiece with them at all times.

If you desire to engage in a particular task and wish to establish a reminder, I recommend setting the alarm to occur 15 minutes prior to the intended time.

Focus on one thing. This will ensure the timely completion of your task.

Examine the duration invested in the preceding tasks to ascertain the amount of time expended and the remaining time required to accomplish the work.

Do not engage in the pursuit of trivial justifications, as no one possesses the ability to fulfill preconceived ideals. As a consequence of this, it will prove to be inefficient.

Please ensure that the tasks are executed based on their respective priorities. Given that each task cannot be accomplished independently, it is advisable to prioritize the significant tasks and defer the remainder until afterwards.

Enlist the assistance of others to carry out the task. Less significant tasks can be delegated to others for their execution. This will enable you to focus on other paramount tasks.

If there exists a similar task to be carried out, it could be undertaken from an intermediate position. Additionally, you have the option to disseminate it among individuals. Subsequently, the task can be effortlessly accomplished.

Engaging in certain activities can be a potential distraction, diverting your focus from the primary task at hand, which holds greater significance.

Adhere to a time interval of 5 to 10 minutes between consecutive tasks, allowing for a sufficient period to complete and submit the initial task.

• Organize your workload in a manner that will bring you satisfaction and contentment.

• Perceive work as a professional endeavor rather than a burden. Do not become agitated in the event that the task remains unfinished for any cause. Consequently, it is probable that you will not be able to complete the subsequent task to the highest degree of perfection.

• Don't get overloaded. Upon the completion of a task, it is advisable not to immediately commence another task.

• Endeavor to undertake all tasks with utmost commitment.

• Engage in your work as a form of devotion.

You must have faith in the knowledge and comprehension gained through your personal encounters.

- Know your excuses. Enhance the standard of one's self-esteem.

- Speak in a hushed manner without causing harm to anyone.

- Refrain from engaging in actions towards others that you would not appreciate being directed towards yourself.

- Acquire proper proficiency in the accurate usage of comprehension and conviction. • Familiarize oneself with the correct utilization of understanding and belief. • Gain knowledge in the appropriate application of understanding and belief. Attentively heed each utterance and place trust cautiously, while harboring a semblance of skepticism within, to safeguard oneself from deceit.

In our world, there exists both virtue and vice. Do not become agitated or anxious by the current circumstances. Proceed towards your goal.

- Every problem has a multitude of potential solutions. Carefully consider the situation from all perspectives. The solution may be concealed in an alternative location.

A Story

In a bygone era, there existed a landowner who found himself in need of financial assistance. The zamindari system has been abolished. Consequently, he was left with sole ownership of a single farm. He visited a local financial institution and made a request for a loan. The lender inquired, "Dear sir, may I kindly inform you that I am engaged in business activities?" You have already derived financial assets through the process of collateralizing the land in your possession. Currently, you do not possess any assets to serve as collateral; therefore, I am unable to extend a loan to you."

The landowner responded, "Sir, I assure you that I will promptly reimburse the funds I have borrowed from you and regain possession of my land within a span of two years." I am planning to travel to the city with the purpose of pursuing financial gain."

The lender stated that he required collateral in order to extend a loan.

The landowner informed him that he possessed no assets except for the dog, therefore suggesting the option of taking the said dog as collateral.

The lender acquiesced to his commitment and provided him with the requisite sum.

The landowner elucidated the circumstances to his canine companion, secured the residence, and departed for the urban center.

One day, the Seth ventured to a neighboring village for business matters, leaving the dog in charge of his residence as a means of security. On that particular day, the residence was unlawfully entered by a group of burglars. The canine experienced a sense of perplexity regarding the course of action it ought to pursue. The perpetrators clandestinely gathered all funds before departing, with the canine discreetly tailing them.

They excavated a cavity within the woodland and concealed all the funds within it. The canine witnessed the entirety of the events and proceeded to reenter the premises with utmost serenity.

Subsequently, Seth arrived and was appalled by the condition of his dwelling. He initiated the thought that the dog had deceived him. The canine commenced vocalizing and pulled forcefully at his traditional Indian garment. He regarded it as a signal. He assembled a group of individuals and proceeded to accompany the canine.

The canine arrived at the woodland and commenced excavation of the soil. Upon witnessing this, all individuals proceeded to excavate the area, shortly thereafter unearthing the financial assets. The owner, Seth, was exceedingly pleased by the unwavering loyalty of the dog, which fostered an increase in his fondness towards the animal.

After a span of two years, the zamindar returned to the estate following a profitable stint in the urban hub. He contemplated the prospect of reimbursing the lender on the following day.

Simultaneously, Seth made the decision to waive the loan that the zamindar had acquired and liberate his dog and land. He transcribed all of this information onto a sheet of paper and affixed it securely around the dog's neck. Seth declared, "You may depart. Your freedom has been granted." You have performed admirably in your service. Proceed directly to your supervisor."

The canine promptly initiated its journey towards the domicile of its owner.

The landowner was approaching to resolve the outstanding loan when he witnessed his canine companion approaching him. He pondered, 'The canine has exhibited betrayal towards me. It has caused great embarrassment to me in the presence of Seth and has been directed back towards me.

He discharged a firearm at the canine without exhibiting any hesitancy or contemplation. The canine endured immense suffering and ultimately succumbed to its demise. The landowner observed the document securely fastened around his neck. After perusing it, he was thoroughly astonished.

www.ingramcontent.com/pod-product-compliance
Lightning Source LLC
Chambersburg PA
CBHW050412120526
44590CB00015B/1939